JELLY IN MY BELLY

FUN poems for KIDS!

by

tom catalano

Violet
Enjoy!! :)

Tom catalano

*To Peggy. Thanks for the inspiration
for the poem, 'Jelly In My Belly' (pg 38).
(Note: Jelly with seeds is
HER preference, not mine!)*

CONTENTS

• • •

Anudder Peanut Butter

There is one food

    I like more than the 'udder,

keep all the rest

    I just LOVE peanut butter.

Put it on bread

    or on toast or a muffin,

I eat it all day

    I just can't get enough in.

"I CAN'T eat my fruit!"

    I'd sure like to shout,

but my tongue is stuck

    to the roof of my mout'!

I wish that I could

    convince Fadder and Mudder

to keep all the rest…

    I'll just take peanut butter!

tom catalano

Sticky Business

One day I stepped on gum

y'know it felt so yucky.

It didn't matter what I did,

my foot was very stucky.

I had no way of knowing

the feeling would be icky.

But I guess I should have known

for gum is really sticky.

And when my foot came loose

y'know I felt so dumb.

Not only was my shoe a mess

but now I had no gum!

tom catalano

Red, White,
And Blueberries

If oranges are orange

    and blueberries blue,

there's something I wonder

    I wish that I knew.

The colors all match

    the fruits that I said,

so why aren't STRAWberries

    REDberries instead?

And I know that grapes

    are both purple and green,

but none of them taste

    like grape jelly I've seen.

Bananas aren't 'yellows'

    and neither's a pear.

There sure are strange names

    for SOME fruits out there!

tom catalano

My Runny Nose

Oh my nose, my runny nose

it is red and sore.

I grab a tissue and I sneeze

and then I blow some more.

I took a breath and then I blew

really, really, hard.

I blew so hard the roof blew off

and landed in the yard.

One more sneeze the walls are gone

and I am all alone.

Just my luck I've sneezed myself

right out of house and home.

● ● ●

You may think that it's a joke

but I don't think it's funny.

I don't think that YOU would like

a nose that's always runny!

tom catalano

Tired

I'm feeling tired

    and I'm moving slow.

I'm crawling along

    like a turtle would go.

I'm slipping and sliding

    without any sound,

I'm just like a snail

    that crawls on the ground.

I'm just like the leaf

    that falls from the tree.

Who's feeling tired?

    Just little slow me.

tom catalano

The Artist

I gathered all my markers

and all my crayons too.

I've got every color

in every kind of hue.

I've got my colored pencils

and charcoal by the score.

I've even got my easel

set up on the floor.

My brush is filled with paint,

my pen is filled with ink,

but I can't start cuz I am not

as ready as you think.

I have all the tools I need,

an empty paper too.

WHAT is it that I should draw?

I haven't got a clue!

tom catalano

My Magic Carpet

I've got a magic carpet

on which I like to ride.

It always comes and gets me

as I wait for it outside.

It takes me to a place where

there's lots to see and do.

While I'm there I always learn

some stuff I never knew.

And when the day is over

my carpet takes me home.

Lots of kids are with me

so I never ride alone.

My carpet is a SCHOOL BUS

which takes me to our school.

And though my carpet may not fly

I think it's pretty cool!

tom catalano

Bossy

My parents are so bossy,

I've got so much to do.

They try and make me take a bath

but I just don't WANT to.

They make me eat my vegetables

BEFORE I get dessert.

And they always get so mad

when I'm playing in the dirt.

Sometimes I have to make my bed

or brush my teeth at night.

I EVEN have to wash my face,

something's just not right.

I wonder if they're bossy

cuz of something that I did.

Perhaps they haven't noticed

that I am just a KID!

tom catalano

Bitter Batter

Betty mixes batter

before she starts to bake.

I like to take a taste

and guess what she will make.

Want to try some batter?

I don't think that you should.

Some think that batter's bitter

I think that batter's good.

It may be bitter batter

that Betty always makes,

but bitter batter's better

once bitter batter bakes.

tom catalano

What?

You said it fastly

    it went right past me

I just didn't hear what you said.

It went in my ear

    but I didn't hear

it just didn't stick in my head.

I hear your voice yapping

    I see your lips flapping

I just do not know what you said.

You must say it slower

    a little bit lower

or I'll have to ignore you instead!

tom catalano

Dots

One day I'm feeling fine,

as happy as can be.

The next thing that I know

there are dots all over me!

Some are on my face

and some are on my nose.

Some are on my back

and some are on my toes.

Some are on my neck

and some are in my hair.

Some are on my legs

— I've got 'em everywhere!

● ● ●

There's a pox upon me

I don't like it one bit.

So many dots are on me

it's difficult to sit.

I'd like to play outside

but I just can't, you see.

In case you haven't noticed...

THERE ARE DOTS ALL OVER ME!

tom catalano

Rain

Sometimes I look up to the sky

> and watch as clouds begin to cry.

Then I wonder what I said

> to make the clouds be sad instead.

And when the rain keeps coming down

> making puddles on the ground

in every puddle I will go

> 'til I am soaked from head to toe.

Sometimes I play the earth will flood

> or I'll make pies made out of mud.

I like to watch the worms come out

> which always makes my sister shout.

Perhaps it isn't tears that fall,

> perhaps the clouds aren't sad at all.

Perhaps it's just for having fun

> on days the sky has lost the sun!

tom catalano

Wyatt Burp

At home they call me Wyatt Burp

    because at dinner I will slurp.

With every drink I take a sip

    I swallow then I let it rip.

You can hear it down the halls

    and it even shakes the walls.

I try and stop but I let loose

    I sound just like a baby moose.

The neighbors call us to complain

    but every meal it's the same.

When I eat you'd best stand back

    I may just have a burp attack.

I don't mean to hurt your ear

    but Wyatt Burp is burpin' here!

tom catalano

Socks And Shoes

Each and every morning

there's something that I do.

I always put a sock on

and then I put a shoe.

Some people put on both

their socks before their shoes,

but I find that it is not

the method that I choose.

Perhaps you never thought

of which you like to do —

first a sock and then a sock

or a sock and then a shoe.

• • •

Getting up tomorrow

before you hit the street

pause for just a moment

and think about your feet.

YOU may find out something

of which you never knew.

Did your socks get put on first

or first a sock then shoe?

That is all I have to say

though I may sound confused.

By now I think you know

I like my socks and shoes!

tom catalano

Little Snowflake

Little Snowflake white and round
floated gently to the ground.
He landed there without a sound
without another flake around.

He looked around but could not see
where the other flakes could be.
Perhaps they're all up in the tree
it really is a mystery.

He looked up, but no flakes there
the branches of the tree were bare.
He knew he shouldn't really care
but where WERE they, oh where, oh where?

● ● ●

The only one that made it down

was Little Snowflake on the ground.

He'd hoped that others were around

together they could make a mound.

Where kids could slide down with a sled

with hats pulled down upon their head

and dream of snowflakes in their bed,

but he lies alone instead.

Little Snowflake had to try

to keep the tears out of his eye.

Then suddenly up in the sky

he saw snowflakes start to fly.

● ● ●

Little Snowflake had to say,

"Goody, yippee, hip hooray,

I've been waiting here all day.

At last we can finally play!"

Snowflakes floated like a feather

looking just like winter weather.

Little Snowflake felt much better

knowing good friends stick together.

tom catalano

I Hate Winter

I must be getting old

for I can't stand the cold

    I know that winter's not my time of year.

The wind will start to blow

and then there's ice and snow

    it makes me want to move right out of here.

I'll move to where it's hot

cuz there is where I'm not,

    I'd sit outside all day with cloudless sky.

That is what I'd do

cuz frankly of the two

    instead of freezing I would rather fry!

tom catalano

I Thought My Brain Liked Me

Last night I had a dream,

    y'know the scary kind.

It really is amazing

    what goes on inside my mind.

I'll have a happy day

    and then I'll go to bed,

but then I have these thoughts

    all going through my head.

I have to fight a monster

    or eat some kind of bug.

Or something in the darkness

    will give my shirt a tug.

Or maybe I get lost

    and can't find my way home.

Or maybe I get scared

    because I'm all alone.

• • •

When I wake next morning

    I just can't help but feel

that it kind of bothers me

    because it seems so real.

The brain that helps me breathe

    and helps me through the day

waits until I fall asleep

    and THEN goes out to play!

I don't know if my brain

    gets bored but NOW I do.

It likes to do the things

    that I just DON'T like to!

tom catalano

The Way I Am

I've got a face

    and I've got a nose.

I've got some feet

    and I've got some toes.

But how they got there

    nobody knows

...that's just the way I am.

I've got two eyes

    and I've got a chin.

I've got some legs

    and I've got a shin.

On top of all that

    I've got this skin

...that's just the way I am.

● ● ●

I've got a mouth

  and I've got some ears.

I've got lashes

  and I've had some tears,

but that's something I

  have known for years

...that's just the way I am.

I don't know what

  I'll grow up to be,

but from everything

  that I can see,

there's a whole lot of

  pieces to me

...and that's the way I am!

tom catalano

Bent Words

A tree will grow wood

like a tree only could

    if the wood of a tree only would.

A rock on a planet

can't be taken for granite

    not even if you try to plan it.

The sea you would see

if you were with me

    is as lovely as any would be.

If I wanted two

I'd ask for it too

    then, who am I giving it to.

Don't be offended

if the words I have bended

    cuz now this poem has just ended.

tom catalano

Time Machine

If I had a time machine

> I know where I might go.

I'd go back to the past with

> all the knowledge I now know.

I'd invent all kinds of stuff

> we now use every day.

I'd be some kind of hero

> and rich in every way.

Folks will think that I'm so smart

> a visionary too.

But I could only visualize

> what I already knew.

There's one thing that I won't know

> if backwards I transcend.

When I come to write this poem

> how will it finally end?

tom catalano

The Pony

Once there was a pony
    who lived out on his own.
He wandered into our backyard
    and called our yard his home.

Sometimes he'd run in circles
    or race in a straight line,
sometimes he'd stand and watch the birds
    as if to pass the time.

We tried to feed him apples
    but he would not come near.
He was apprehensive but
    there was no need to fear.

• • •

We cared for his well-being

    his trust we hoped to get.

But he rejected saddle

    and wouldn't take the bit.

We left the apples on a plate

    to show him that we care

and he would always eat them up

    but when we were not there.

One day we brought the apples out

    he was waiting at that place.

He stuck his neck out far enough

    for us to stroke his face.

At last we knew we'd earned his trust

    it was a special day,

but early the next morning

    that pony ran away.

● ● ●

I guess some things just can't be changed

some things were meant to be.

A pony came to teach us

some things are best left free.

tom catalano

I Wish
I Had Wishes

I wish I had wishes

    I wouldn't do dishes no more.

I don't mind mowin'

    the grass that is growin' outdoor.

I don't mind moppin'

    the food that is droppin'

    or sweepin' the dust on the floor.

But I don't like dishes

    so I'll just make wishes

    that I don't do dishes no more!

tom catalano

The Lawn
On My Head

One day I looked outside

    and saw the grass out there

and then I started thinking

    how grass is like our hair.

Some lawns are oh so lush,

    well-trimmed and oh so green

they complement the landscape

    the loveliest you've seen.

Grass will just keep growing

    unless it gets a trim

and if it gets neglected

    it WILL begin to thin.

● ● ●

So take care of the grass

    that's growing way out there

or you may have a lawn

    with patches that are bare!

tom catalano

Jelly In My Belly

Give me jelly that has seeds

cuz that is something jelly needs.

Grape is something I don't do

cuz I need something I can chew.

Don't give me peach or apricot

those jellies I don't like a lot.

I would rather have strawberry

or maybe even some raspberry.

Those jellies I will beg for more

cuz seedless jelly is a bore.

There's ONE thing I must confess

that sometimes jelly is a mess.

● ● ●

My teeth get seeds stuck in between

it sometimes makes me want to scream.

For you, this jelly may annoy

but it's the way that I enjoy.

So you can keep your boring grape

and I will take the one that's great.

The one that's mixed with lots of seeds

cuz that is what good jelly needs!

tom catalano

How To Make A Friend

Tell me how you make a friend

— with flour, eggs, and batter?

THIS is how you make a friend

the only things that matter.

You mix a little kindness

and add a bit of sharing

blend in common interest

and stir in lots of caring.

So making friends is easy

and it's something you can do.

Every time you make a friend

they're making one with YOU.

tom catalano

All About
My Poetry

I'm all about my poetry

    it's all about me too.

Things I like to dream about

    or things I like to do.

Places that I've visited

    or places I would go.

Things I like to think about

    or things I think I know.

Some people who I may have met

    or wish that I could see.

My poems may seem familiar

    cuz my poems are part of me.

tom catalano

The Wish List

Little Katie sat alone

    just making out her list.

She even checked the catalog

    to see what she had missed.

There were oh so many toys

    that filled up every page,

things for every boy and girl

    no matter what their age.

She'd take the list to Santa

    and maybe she'd receive

all the presents on her list

    when he came Christmas Eve.

● ● ●

A bike, a ball, and some new clothes,

some crayons, and a pet.

A book, a puzzle, and a game,

whatever she could get.

Her mother took her to the mall

and Santa she would meet,

and sitting in a velvet chair

was Santa in his seat.

The line was long, she'd have to wait,

excitement filled the air.

She could almost read the mind

of every child there.

There was a boy behind her

just standing with his dad.

And what she overheard them say

made her very sad.

● ● ●

"Don't ask Santa for a lot,"

　　the father told his son.

"If Santa brings us presents

　　he'll likely just bring one."

The boy just told his father

　　"I won't make a fuss.

I know that we don't have a lot

　　at least we still got us."

When Katie sat on Santa's lap

　　she whispered in his ear.

She whispered very quietly

　　so no one else would hear.

Then Santa took her list and smiled

　　and sent her on her way.

Her mother couldn't wait to hear

　　what Katie had to say.

● ● ●

"I think that Santa's going to get

me what I want this year.

I just hope that he recalls

what I whispered in his ear.

When I gave my list to him

I said I think it's fine

if he gives what's on the list

to the boy who's next in line."

tom catalano

 **From the author...**

"I hope you have enjoyed reading the poems in this book. I enjoyed writing them.

I believe that poetry should be fun. Fun to read and fun to write.

There are many types of poems. I prefer to write ones that rhyme. I like the challenge of finding just the right rhyming word to tell my story. I find that they flow easily for the reader and for the listener. And for me, that adds to the enjoyment.

It doesn't matter what you write about or how you write it. What matters is that you try. So grab a pencil and paper and write your own poem about something you like, or dislike, or wonder about. You will discover just how fun poetry can be!"

tom catalano

OTHER BOOKS BY TOM CATALANO:

- **Rhymes For Kids!** - Chock full of silly feel-good rhyming poems that kids enjoy. Read them aloud and smile, smile, smile! Includes: *I Wish I Was A Pizza, Bubble Trouble, All God's Critters, Christmas Rap, My Friend Mary-Jean*, and the popular *Cute Little Birdie*. 48 pgs. **$6.95** (ISBN 978-1-882646-05-0)

- **Rhymes For TEENS** - Rhyming poems that don't take themselves too seriously. Will have pre-teens, teens, and adults smiling and feeling good. Includes: *I Survived Elementary School, Stinky Feet, Me Me Me, I Drempt I Was You*, and the patriotic *9-11-01*. 80 pgs. **$9.95** (ISBN 978-1-882646-48-7)

- **Poems For His Glory** - Expect to feel God's presence while reading these faith-inspiring poems. (i.e. *Hope, Heaven, A Cross To Bear, Repaid*). Reviews by Sr. Ann Shields - international evangelist; and Rev. Malachi Van Tassell — Pres., St. Francis University. 96 pgs. All ages. **$9.95** (ISBN 978-1-882646-09-8)

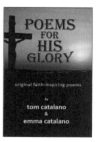

- **Poetry 'N Motion** - Rhyming poems to make you laugh, tug your heartstrings, lighten your day, and entertain you. Includes Christmas poems. Favorites include *Hapless Handyman, Golfer's Lament, Beside Me All The Way*, and *Christmas With Dad*. 96 pgs. Teens-adult. **$9.95** (ISBN 978-1-882646-03-6)

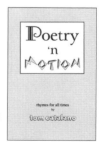

More books on next page!

OTHER BOOKS BY TOM CATALANO:

- **Verse Things First** - Rhyming poems that will tickle your funny bone (i.e. *Coffee Crutch, Wiseacre Novelty Park, This Kitchen*), give you warm and fuzzies (i.e. *First Love, For You*), and move you (i.e. *The Brace, The Mission*). Many poems about Christmas. Very popular. 96 pgs. Teens-adult. **$9.95** (ISBN 978-1-882646-43-2)

- **Rhyme & Reason** - The author's first book. Funny and sentimental rhyming poems on a variety of everyday subjects. Includes *A Child's Christmas, Work Dreams, Las Vegas Vacation of Mine, Wanderlust*, and *Pearanoid*. 96 pgs. Teens-adult. **$9.95** (ISBN 978-1-882646-07-4) Note: A few poems have strong language.

- **I Dig Mud & Yellow Blood** - Funny and touching poems about Caterpillar (the heavy equipment manufacturer), dealers, and the people who use their products. Who would have thought that the construction industry could be so funny...and accurate? 48 pgs. Teens-adult. **$6.95** (ISBN 978-1-882646-91-3)

- **Tall Tales & Short Stories** - 13 original short stories. Some are heartfelt, others are urban science fiction in the style of Twilight Zone. Favorites include *Something's In The Basement, Widowmaker, Telephone Madness, Clementine's Yard,* and *The Carrier*. 176 pgs. Teens-adult. **$10.95** (ISBN 978-1-882646-16-6)

Available through Amazon or contact us:
catalano.tom@gmail.com